This Coloring Book Belongs To:

_____

©2020 Dariusz Radecki
All Rights Reserved

Blobfish
Winner of "The Ugliest Animal on Earth" Award.

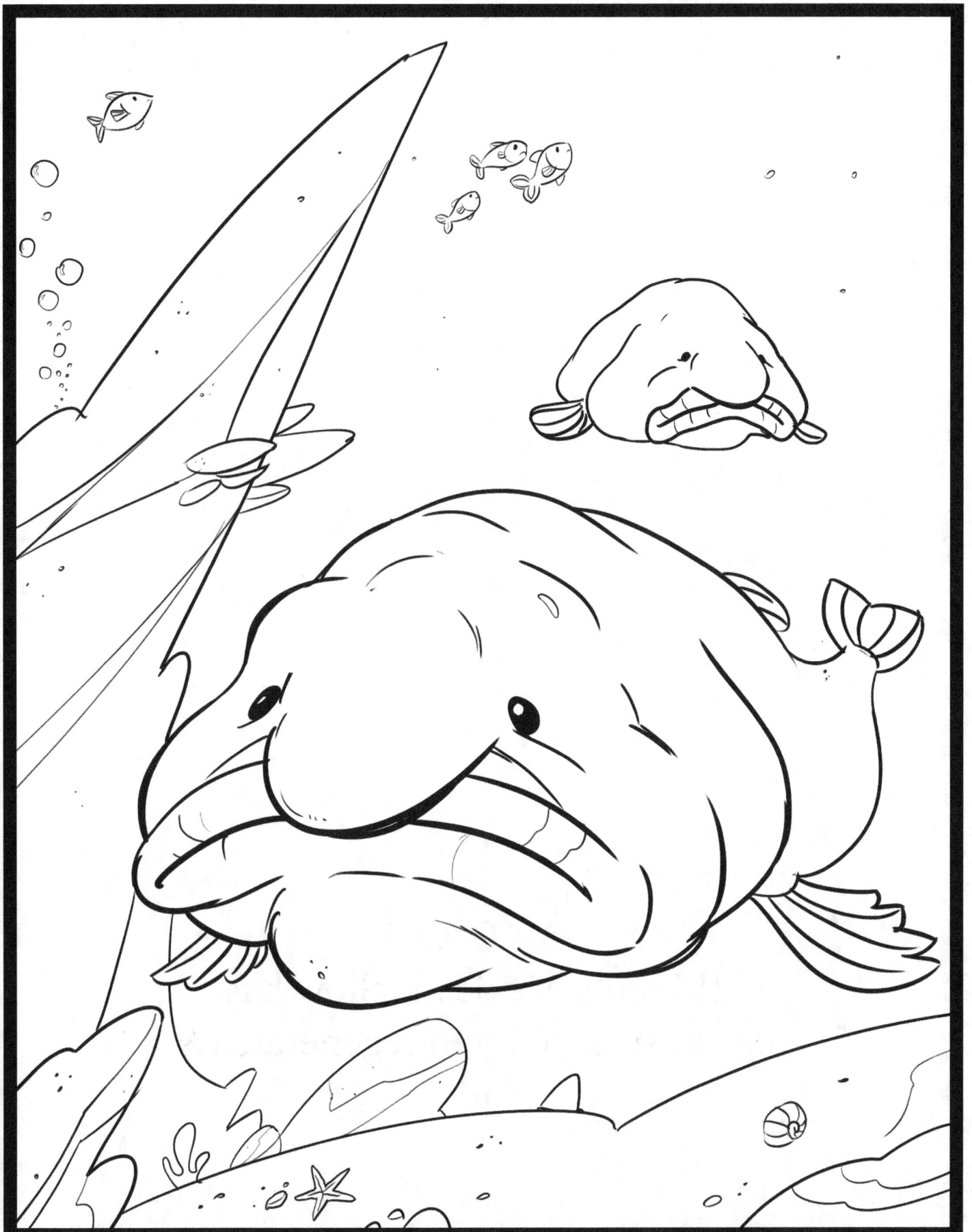

Axolotl
This cute Mexican fellow has impressive ability to regenerate it's body.

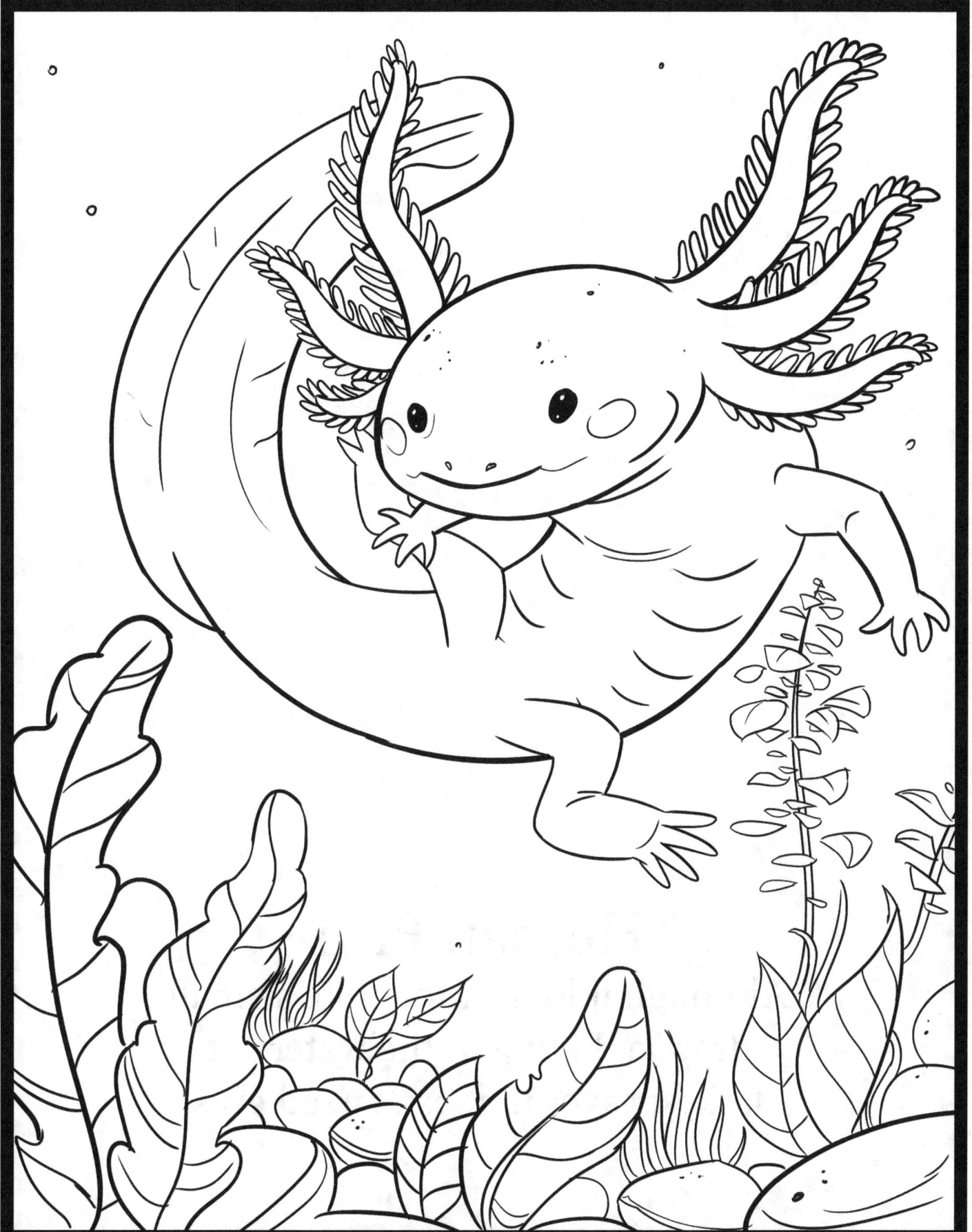

Human Fish
Although it looks more like a small dragon. Living in the waters of darkest caves it doesn't need eyes.

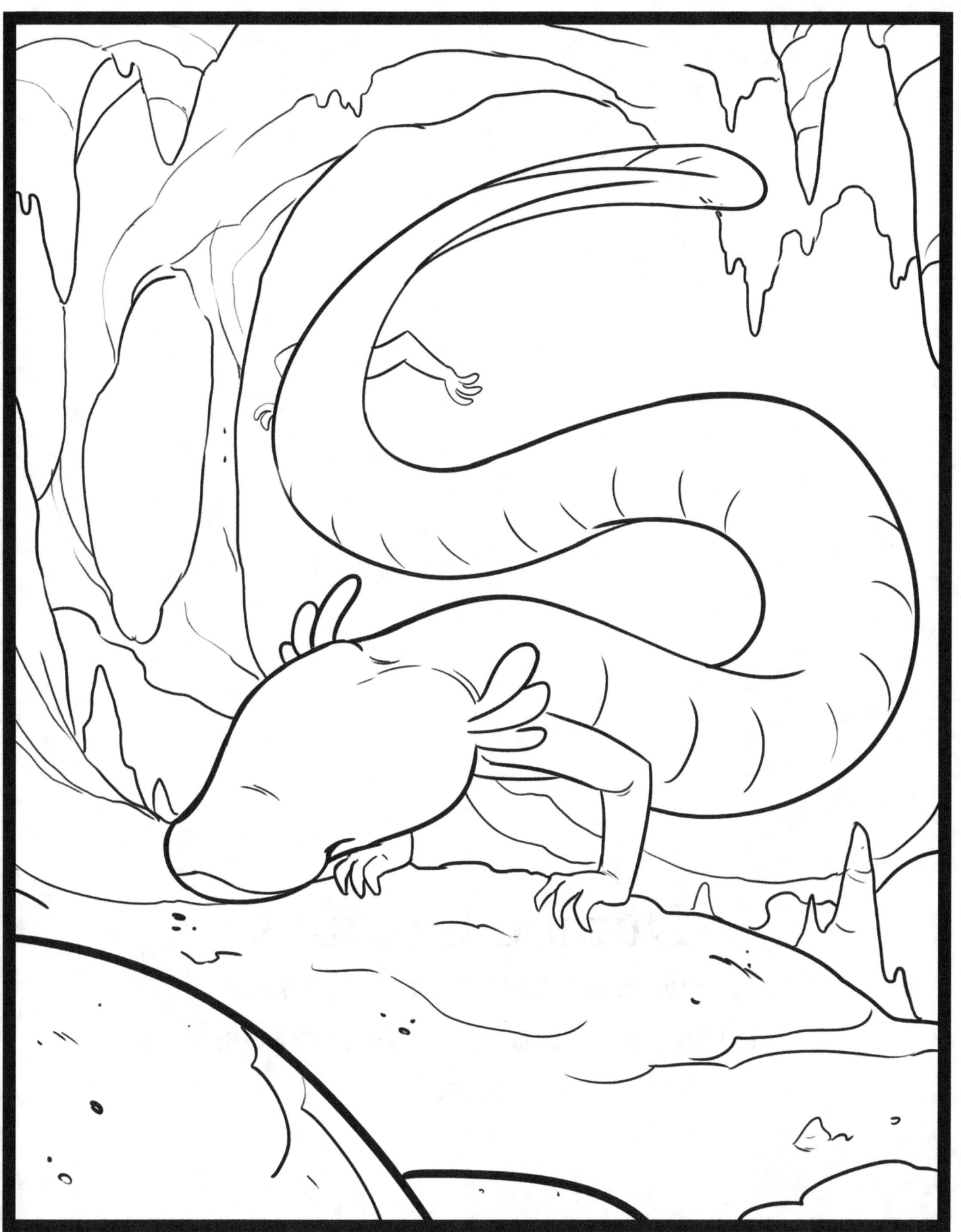

Dumbo Octopus
It owes it's name to the famous Elephant, thanks to characteristic fins.

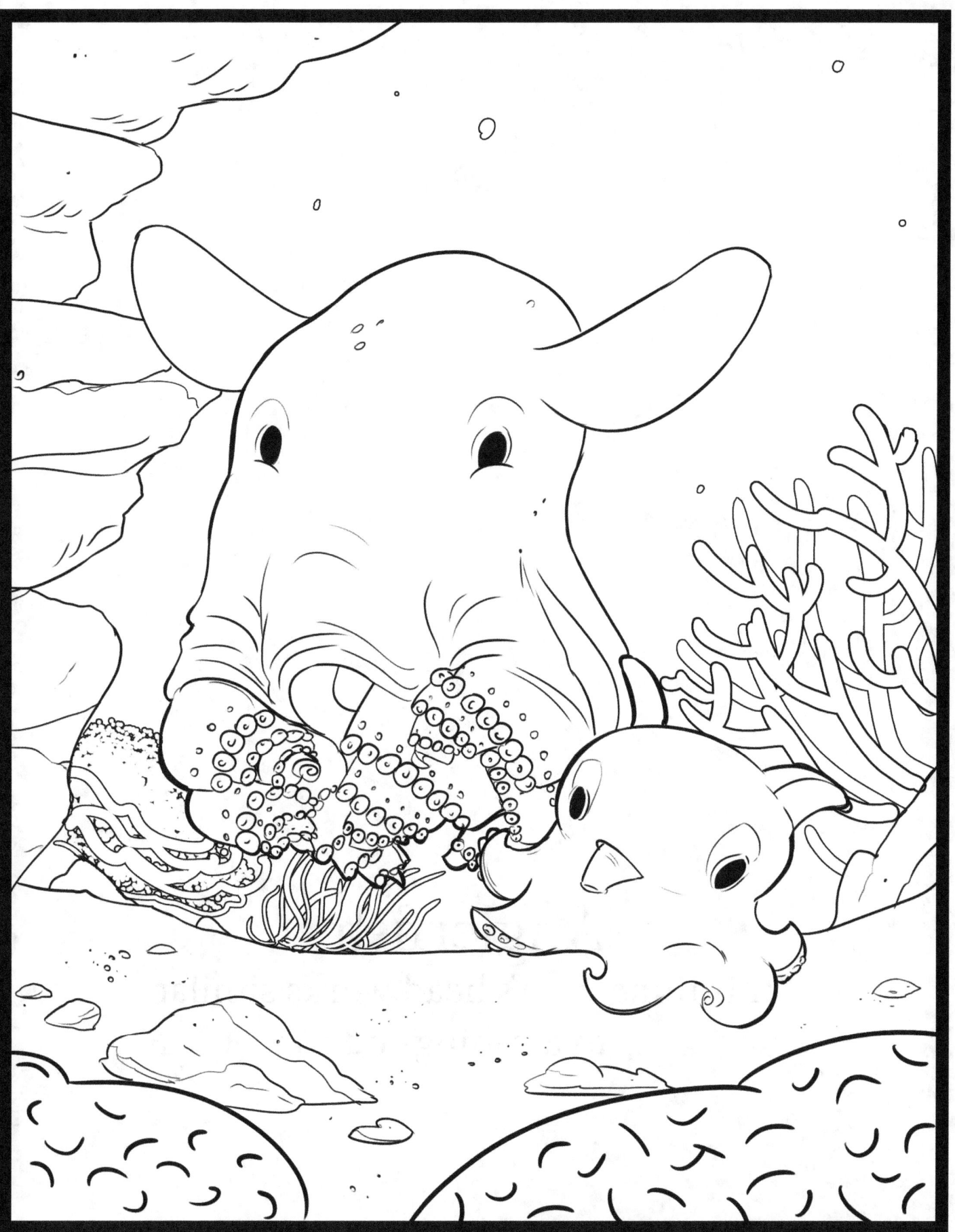

Anglerfish
This thing on it's head works similar to a fishing rod.

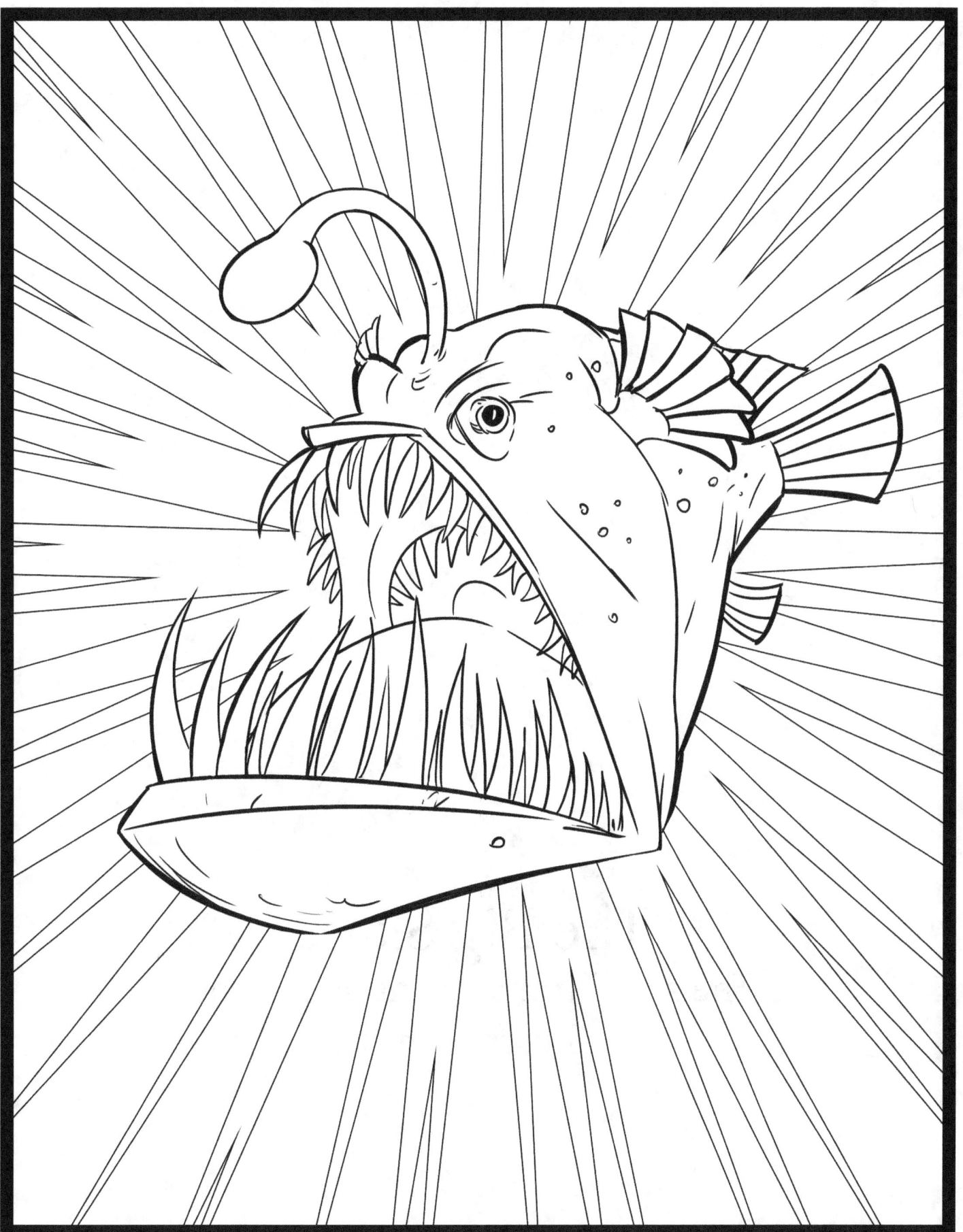

The Big Skate
The small transparent one in the illustration :)

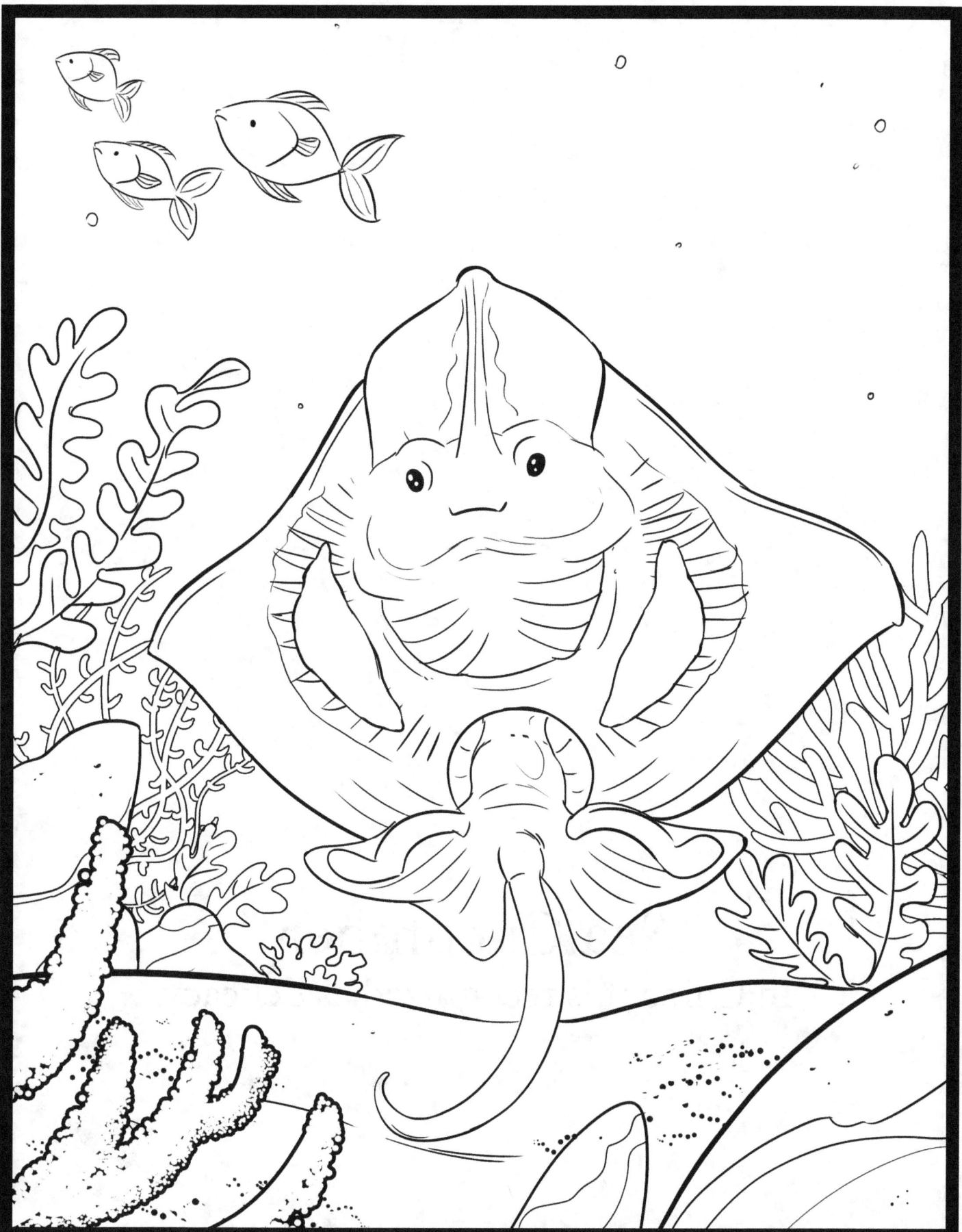

Sea Cucumber
In China it is recognized as delicacy.

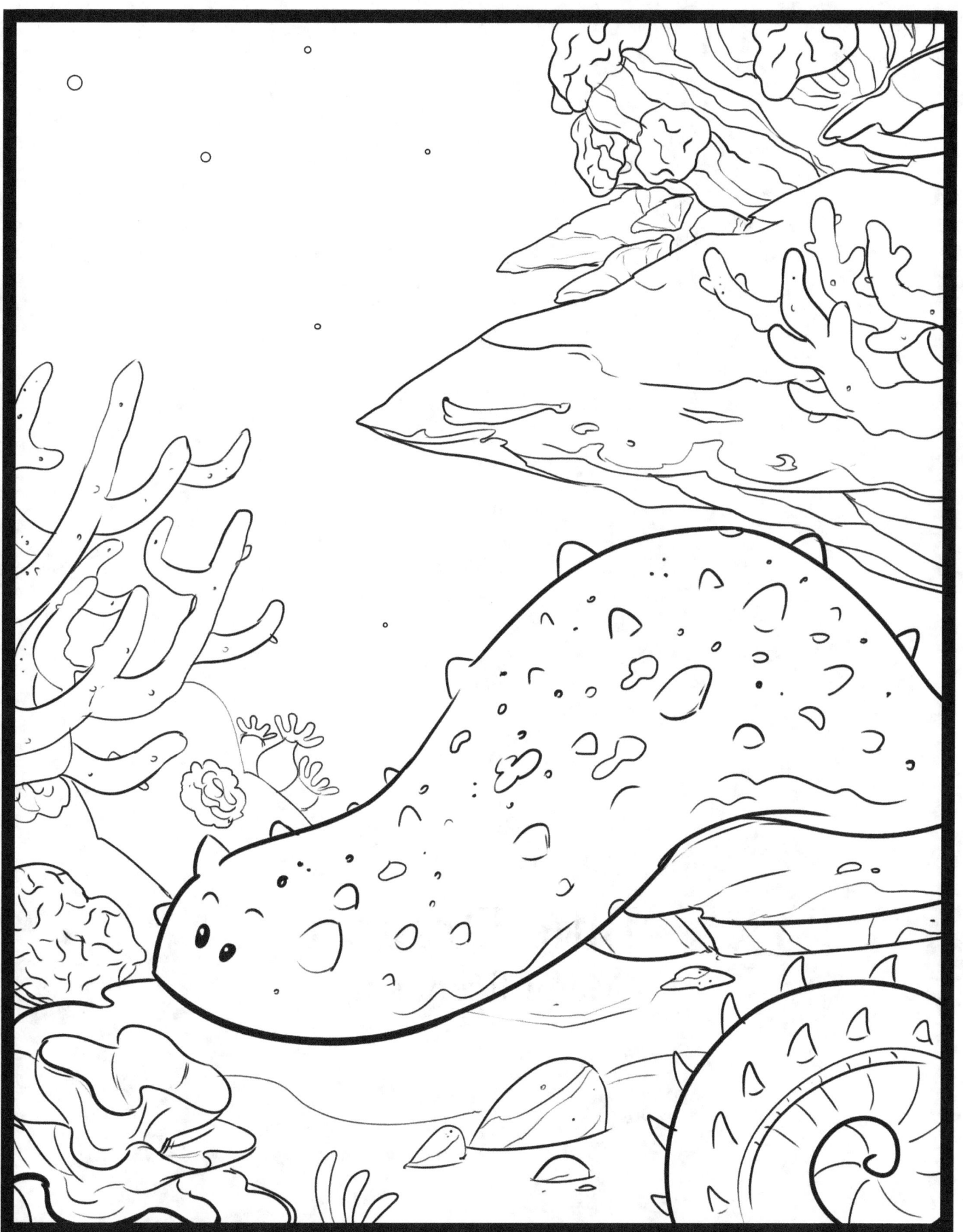

Blue Dragon
Magnificent slug.

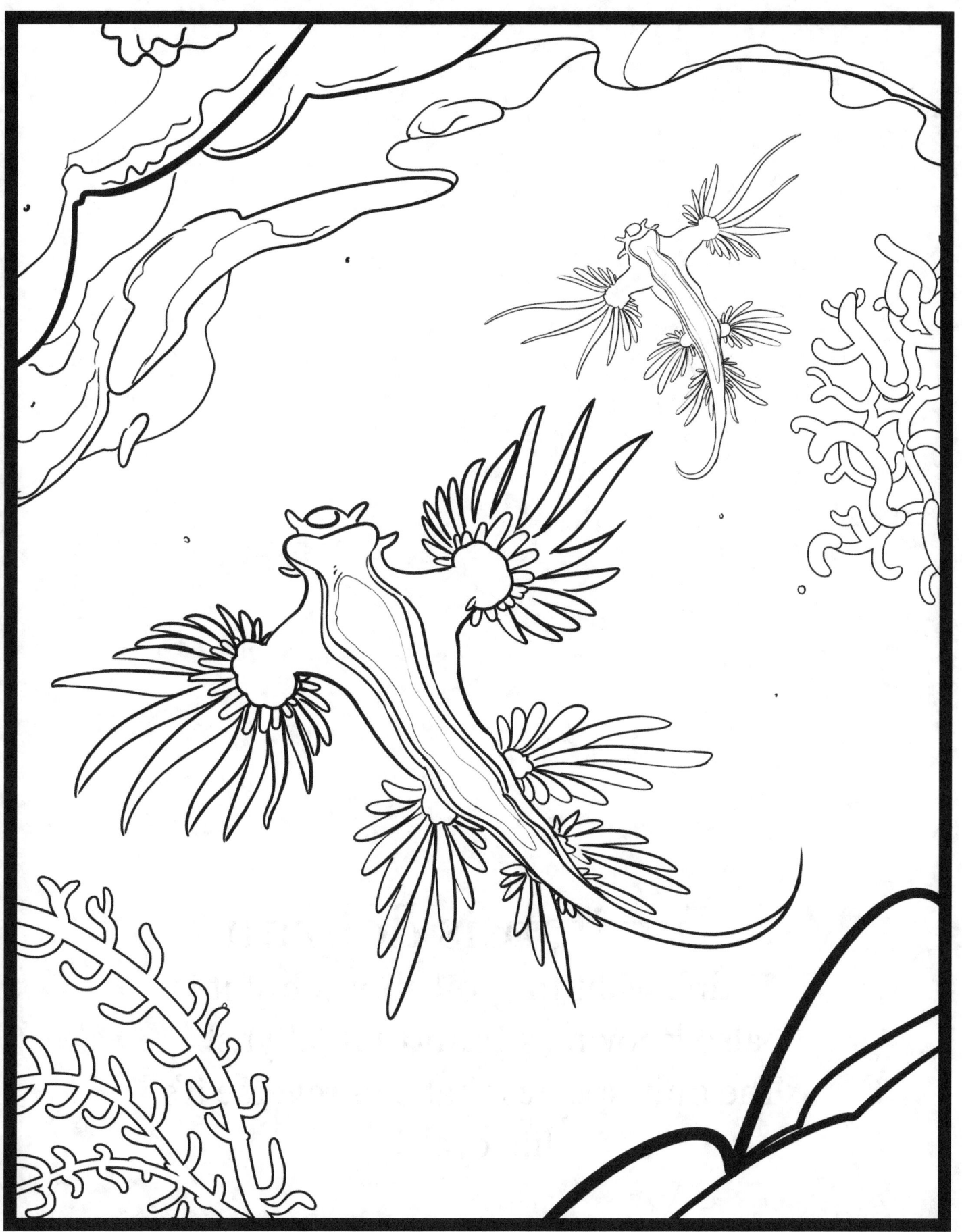

Turritopsis dohrnii
Didn't want to spoil above, but it is also known as Immortal Jellyfish. The only species that can reverse it's life cycle.

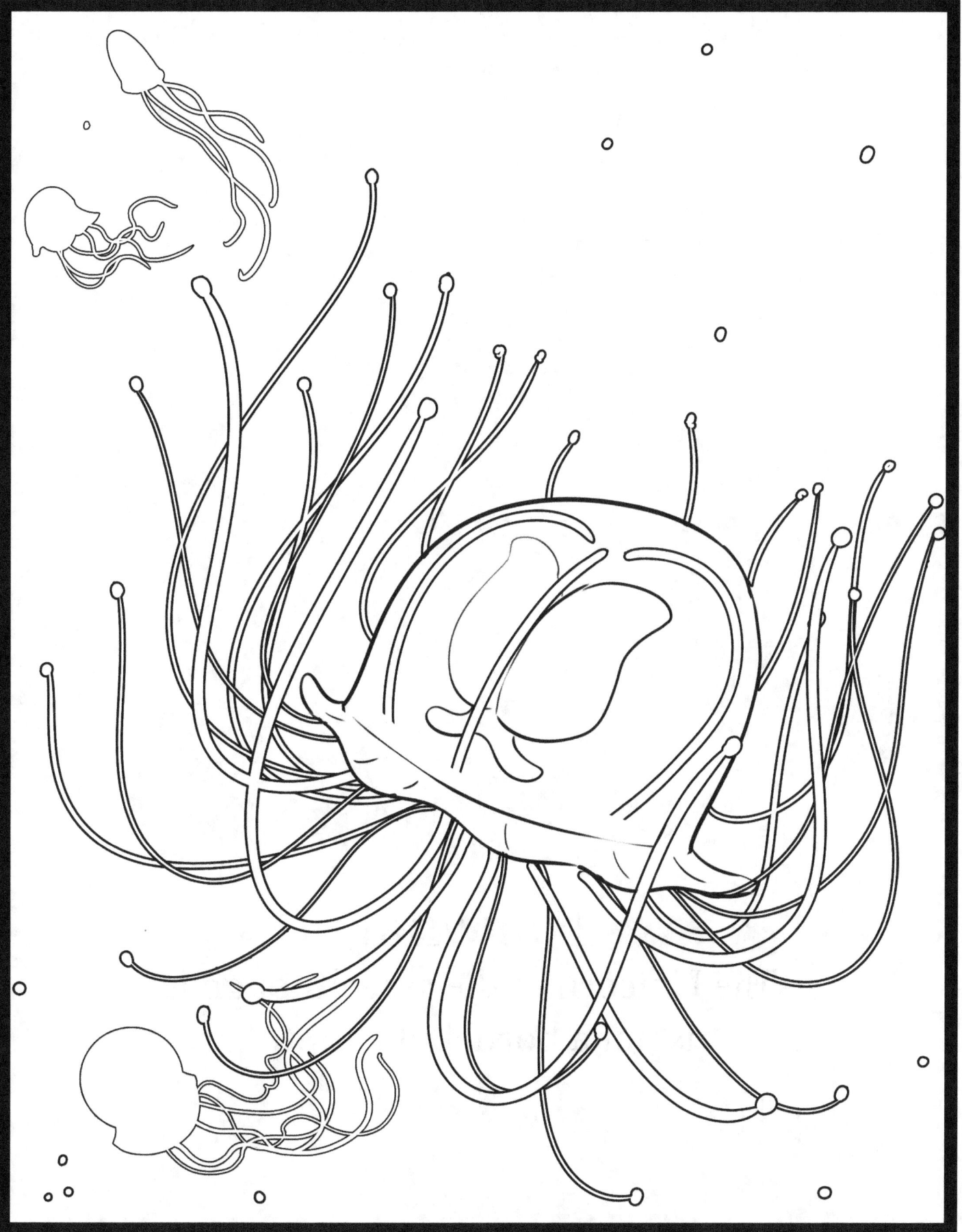

Narwhal
The Unicorn of the sea, although it is not a horn, but a tooth.

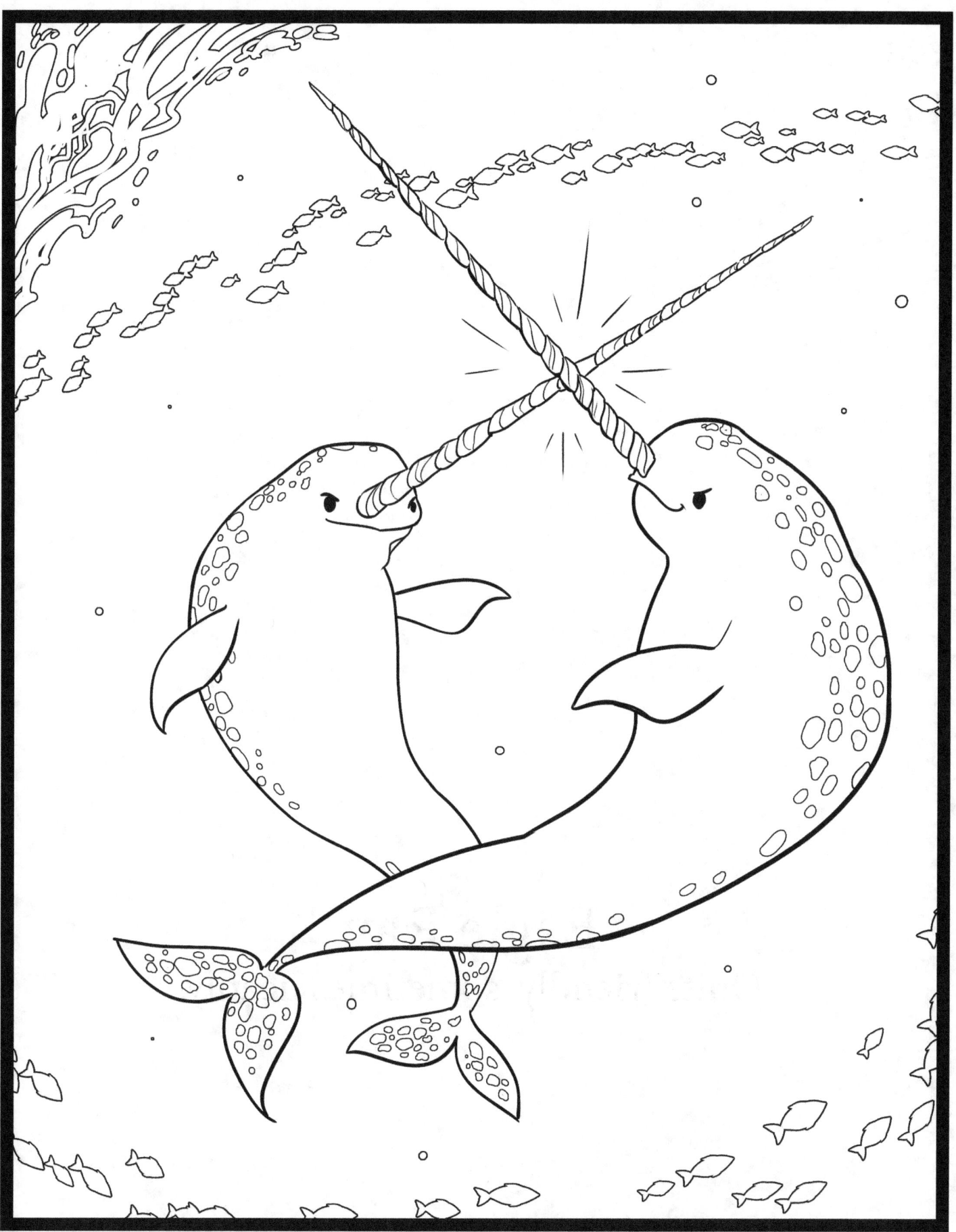

Eagle Ray
Quite friendly, sometimes deadly.

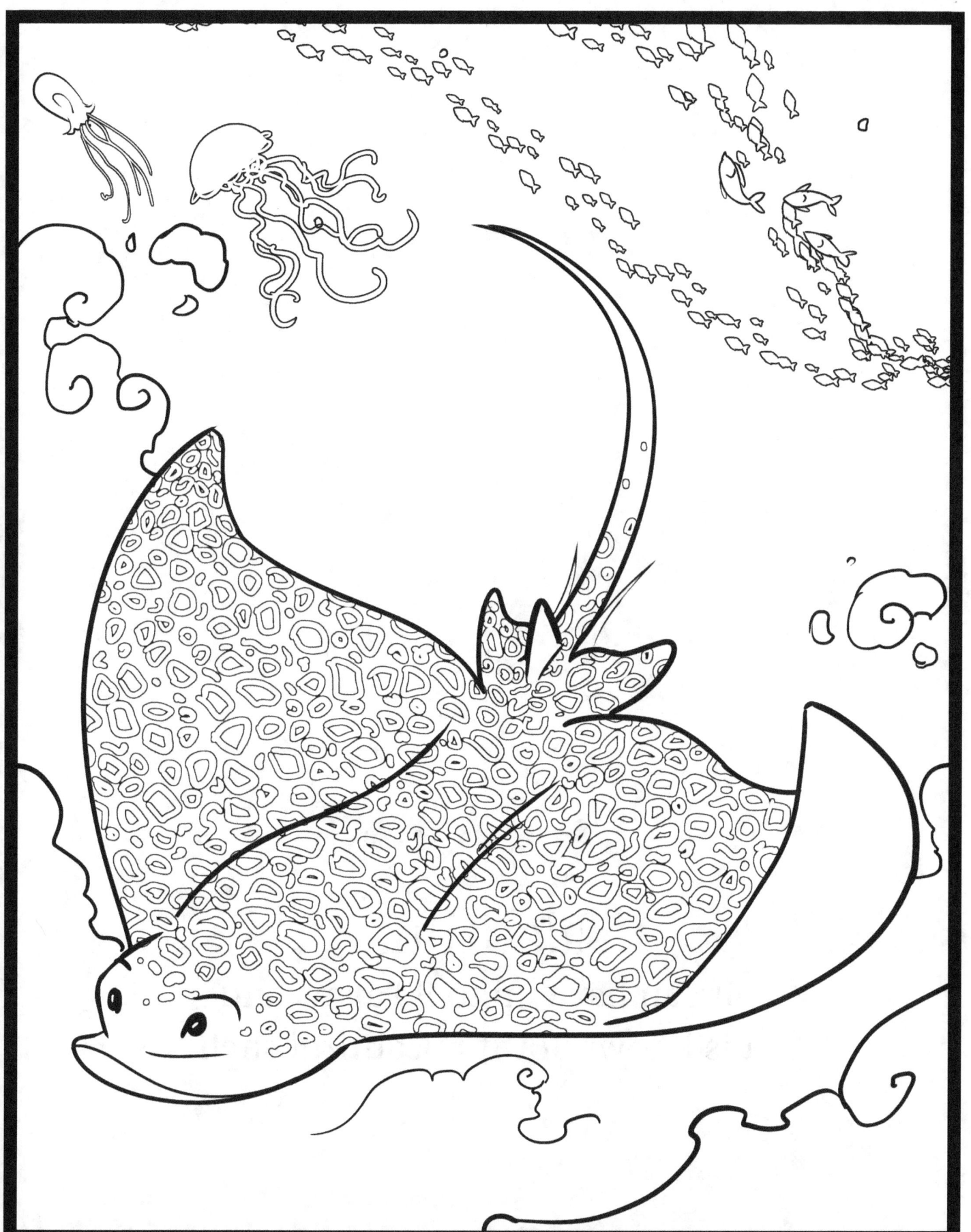

Nautilus
It can have up to 90 arms and
it is known for it's beautiful shell.

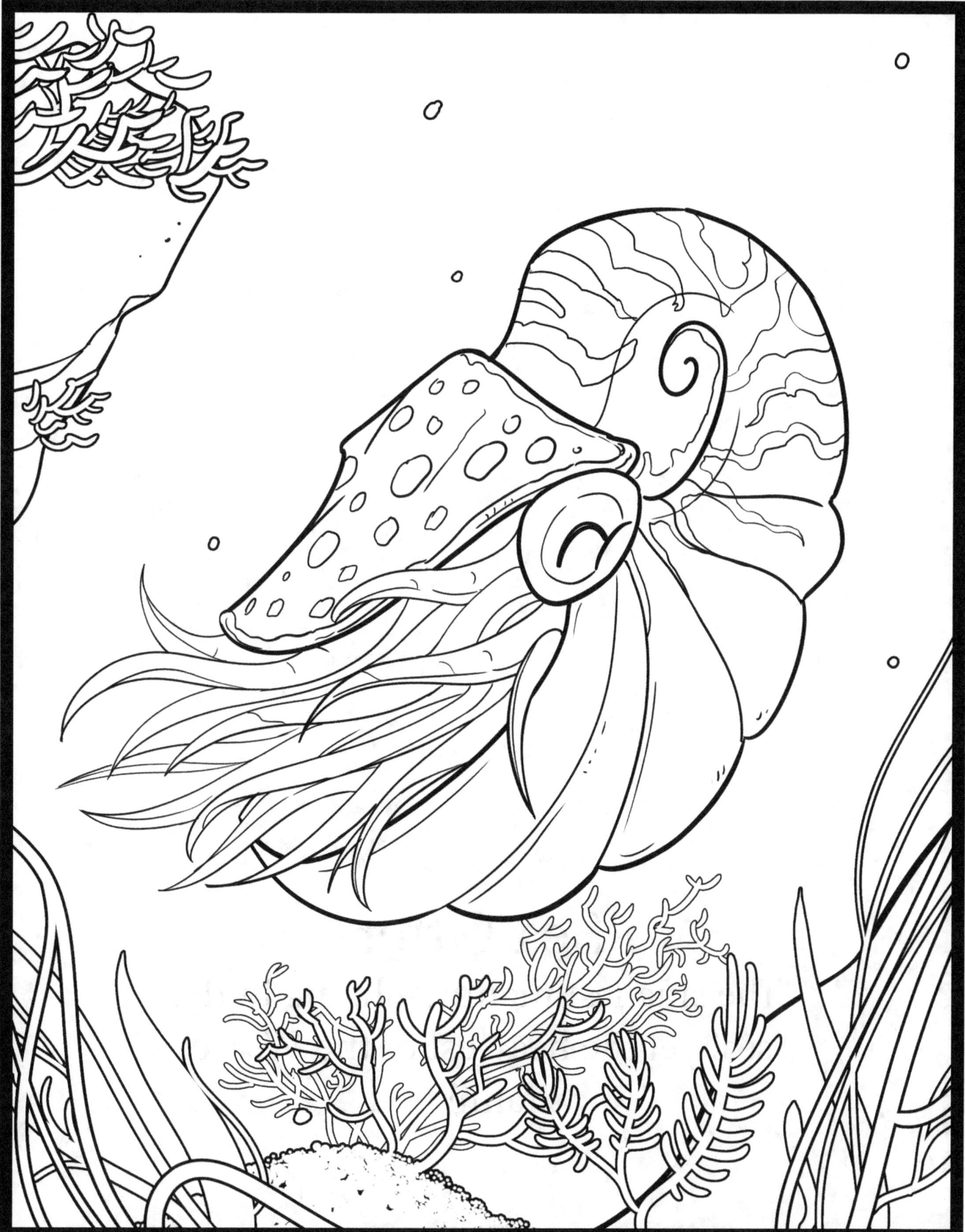

Sea Otter

The smallest mammal living in the sea, yet the heaviest of the Weasel family.

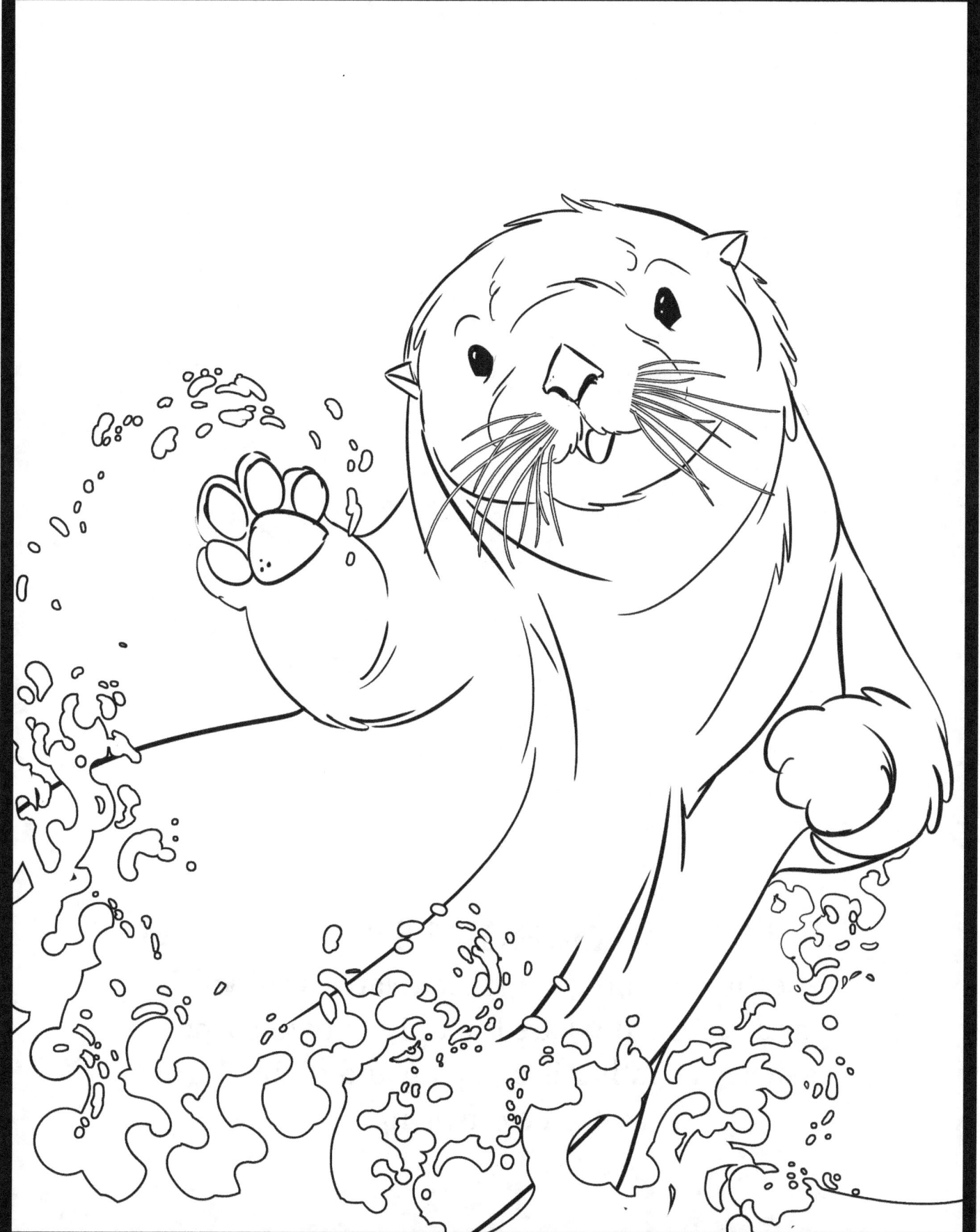

Seahorse

Seahorses and their close relatives (pipefish and seadragons) are the only known species where the father is carrying and giving birth to the offspring.

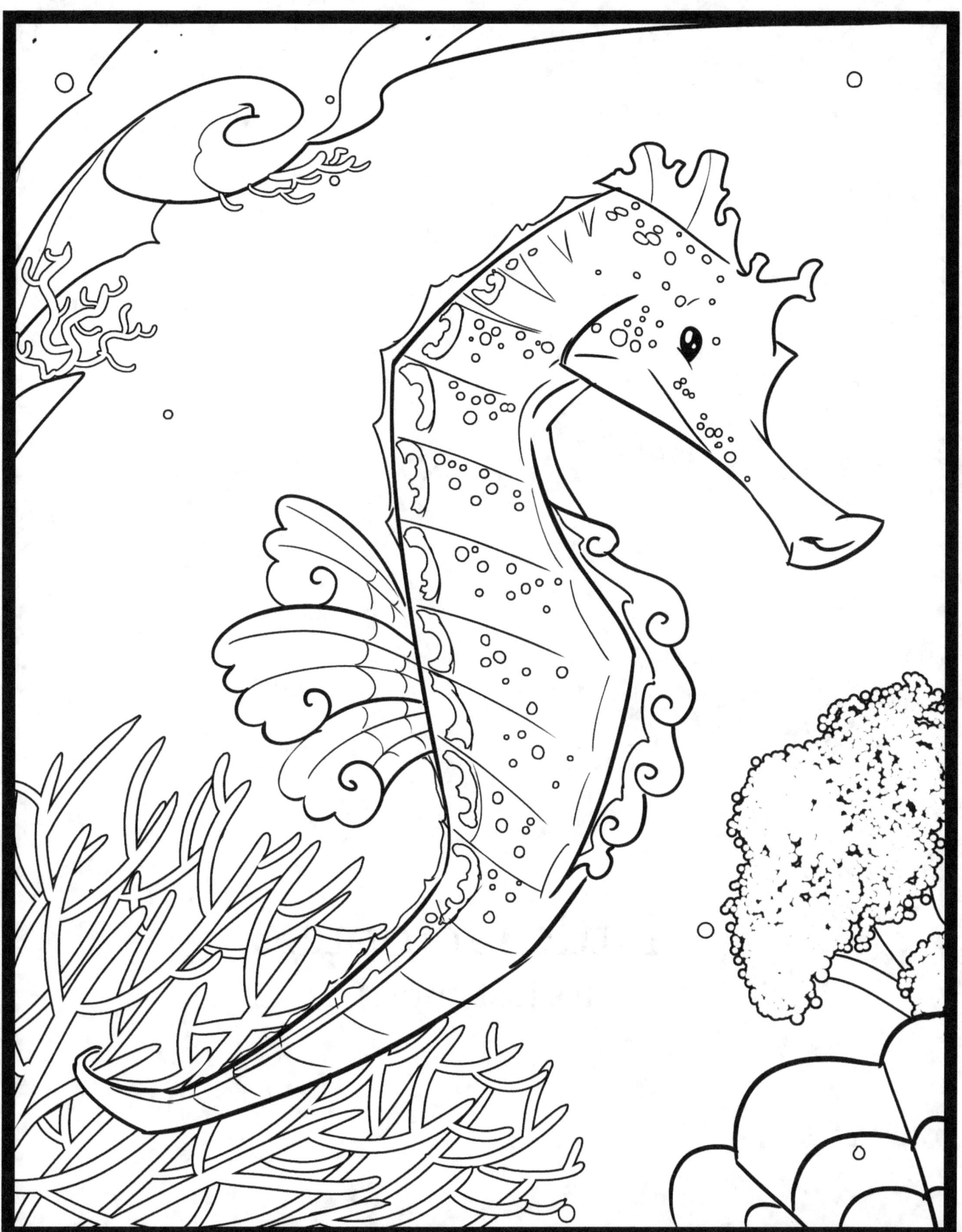

Little Octopus
It's just cute :)

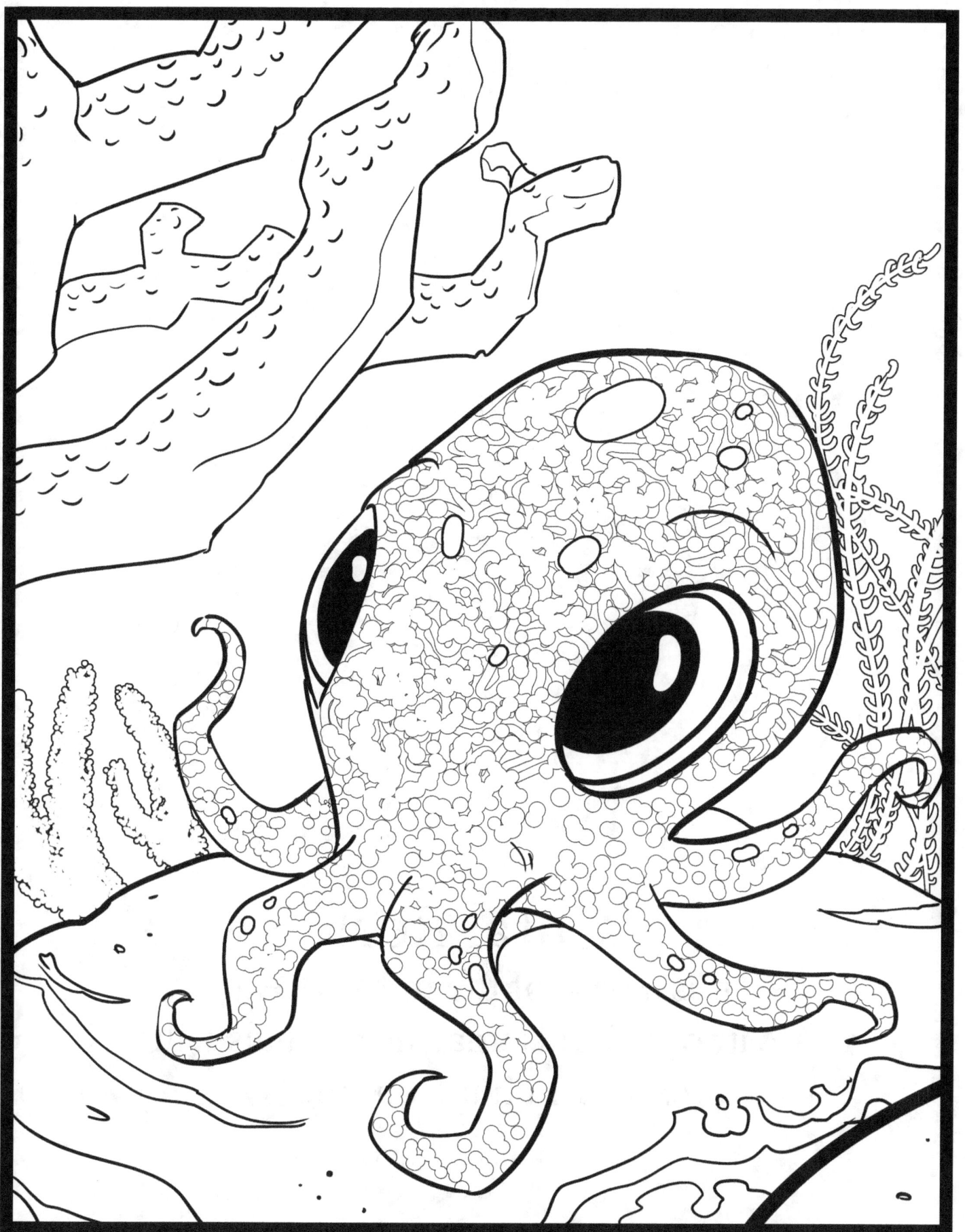

Coral Reef

It is a base of life in the ocean.
Without Corals, marine animals will
extinct in huge numbers.

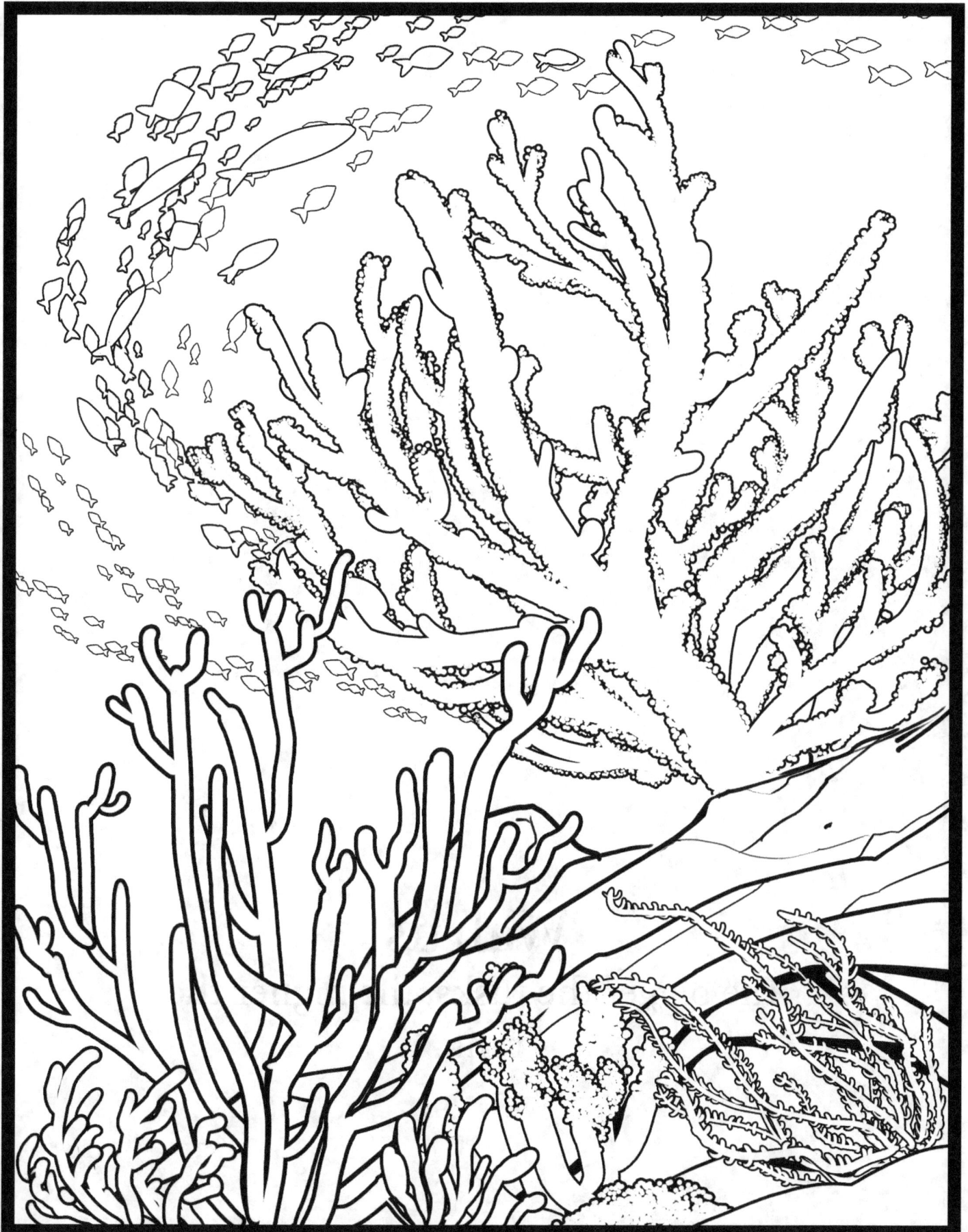

Walrus
The bigger the tusks, the higher the rank.

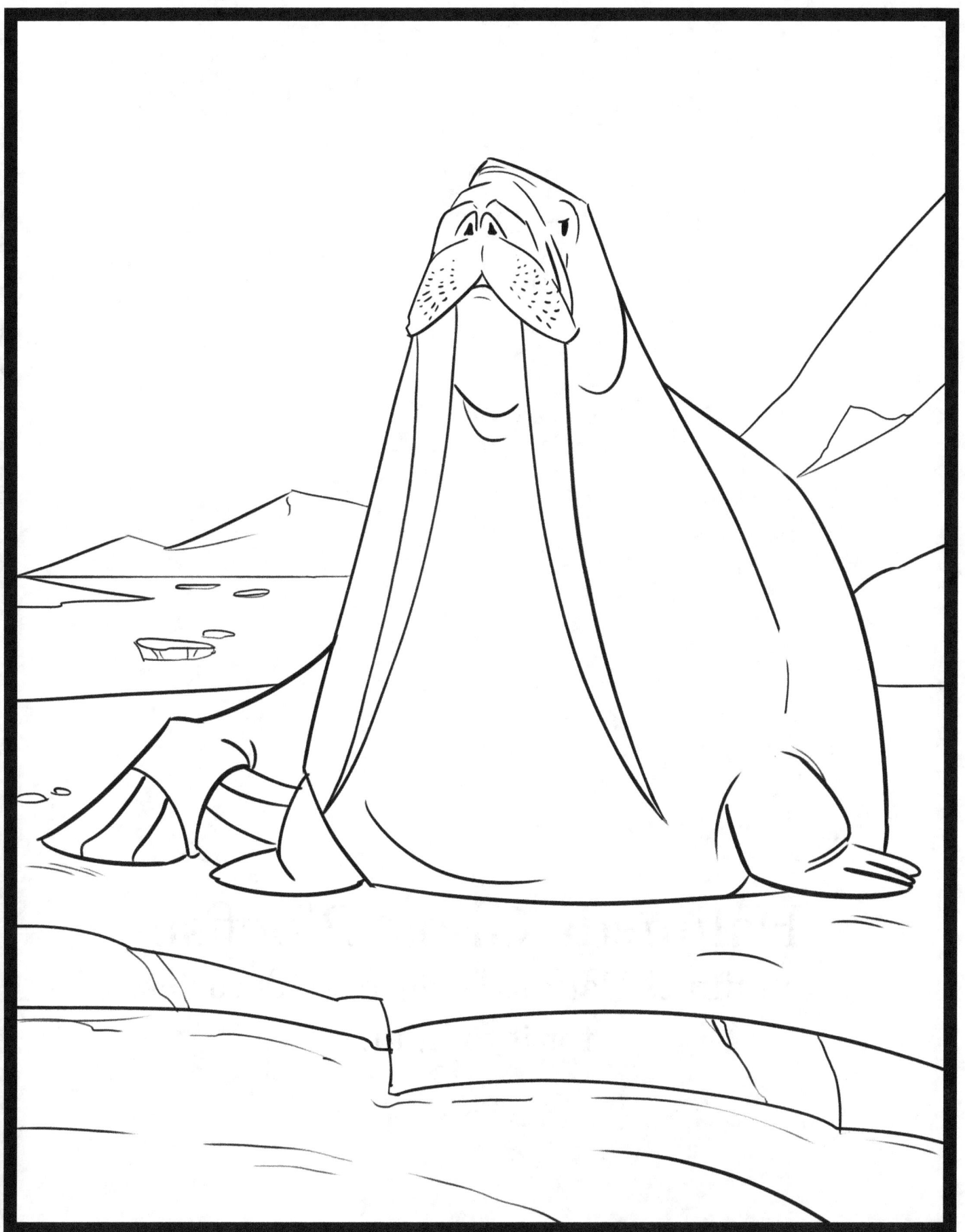

Halimeda Ghost Pipefish
It mimics Halimeda algae so it's easier for it to hunt.

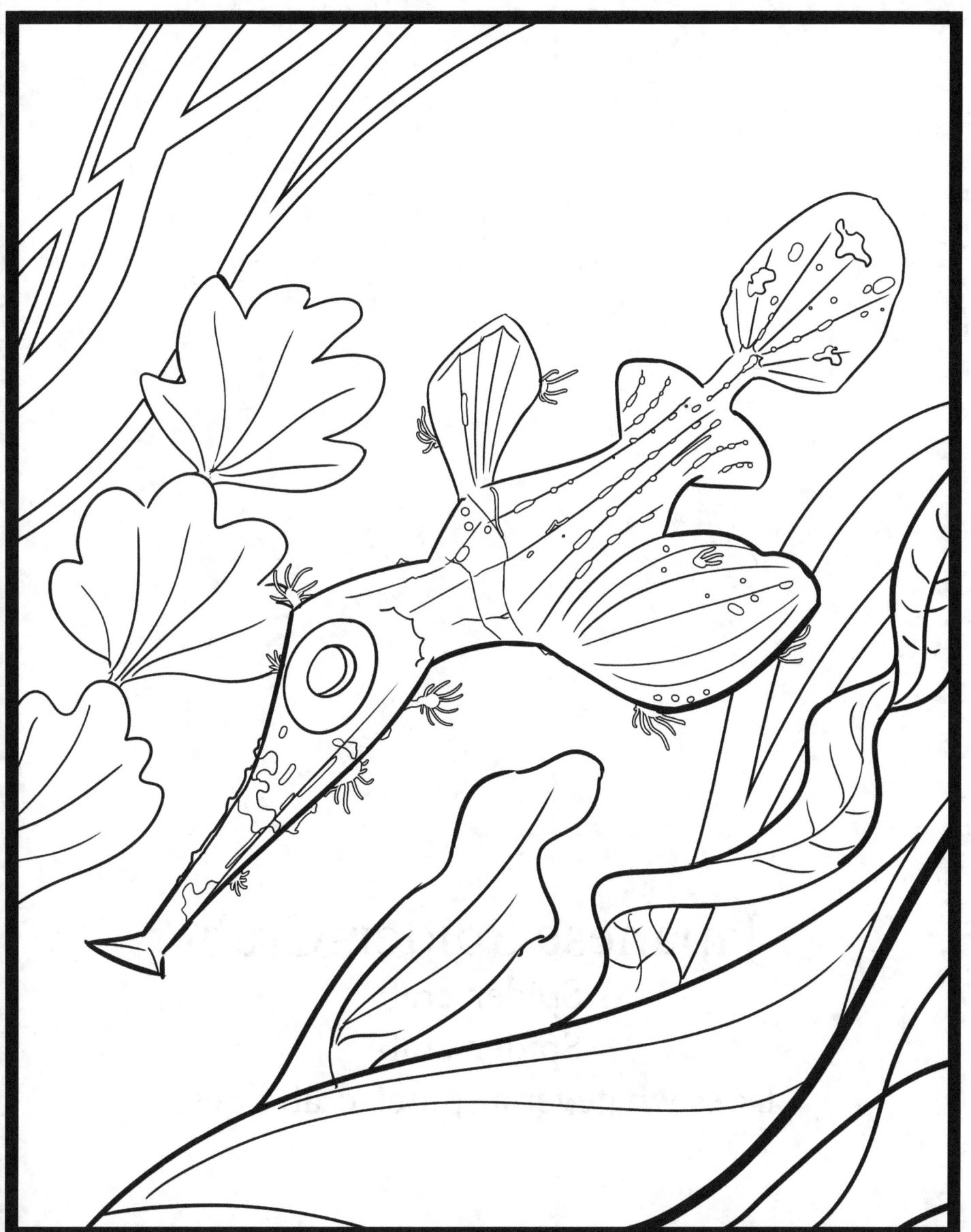

Japanese Spider-Crab
Spider-crab
Spider-crab
Does whatever a spider-crab does.

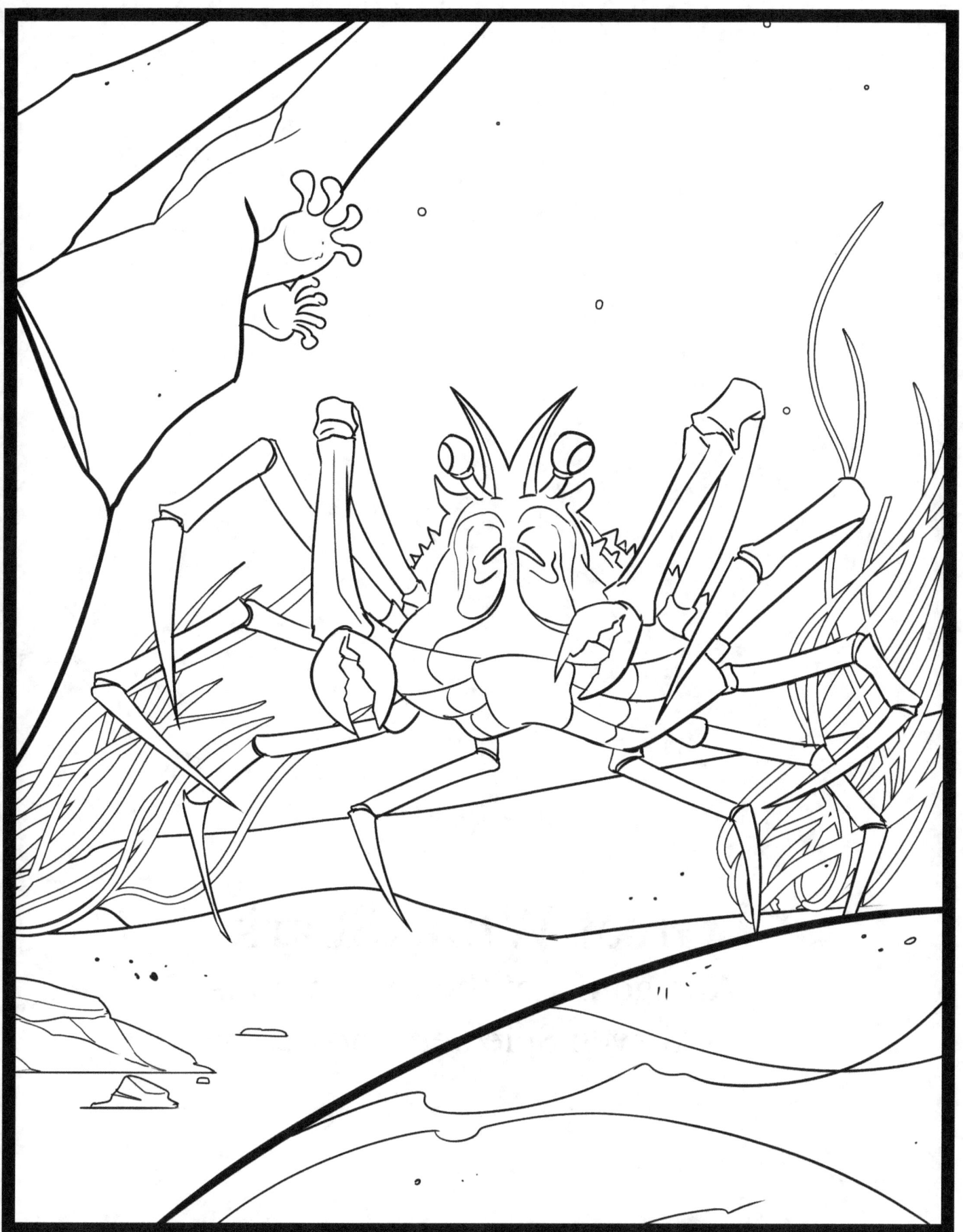

Great White Shark
Antagonist of the very famous
Steven Spielberg movie.

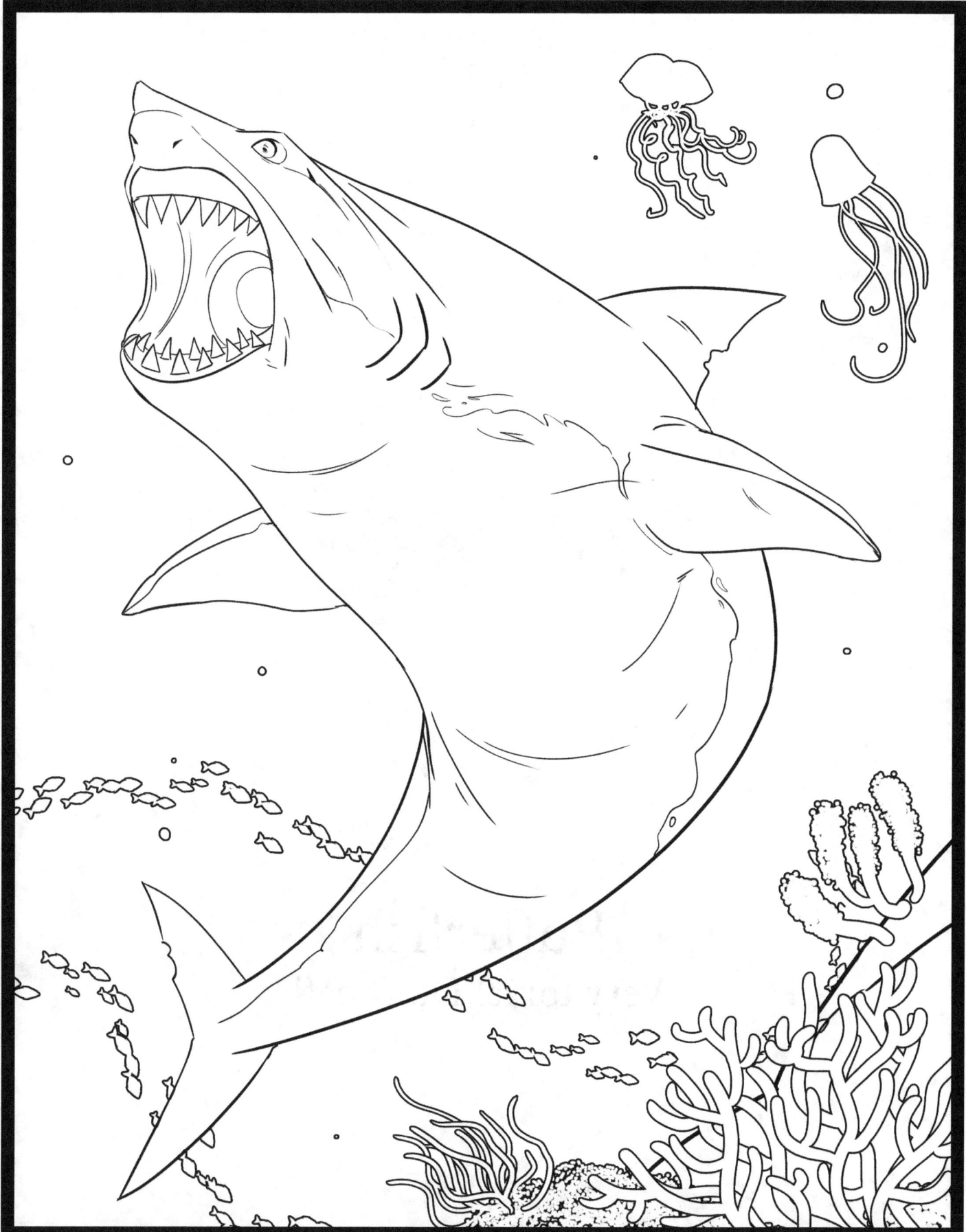

Pufferfish
Very toxic! Don't eat!

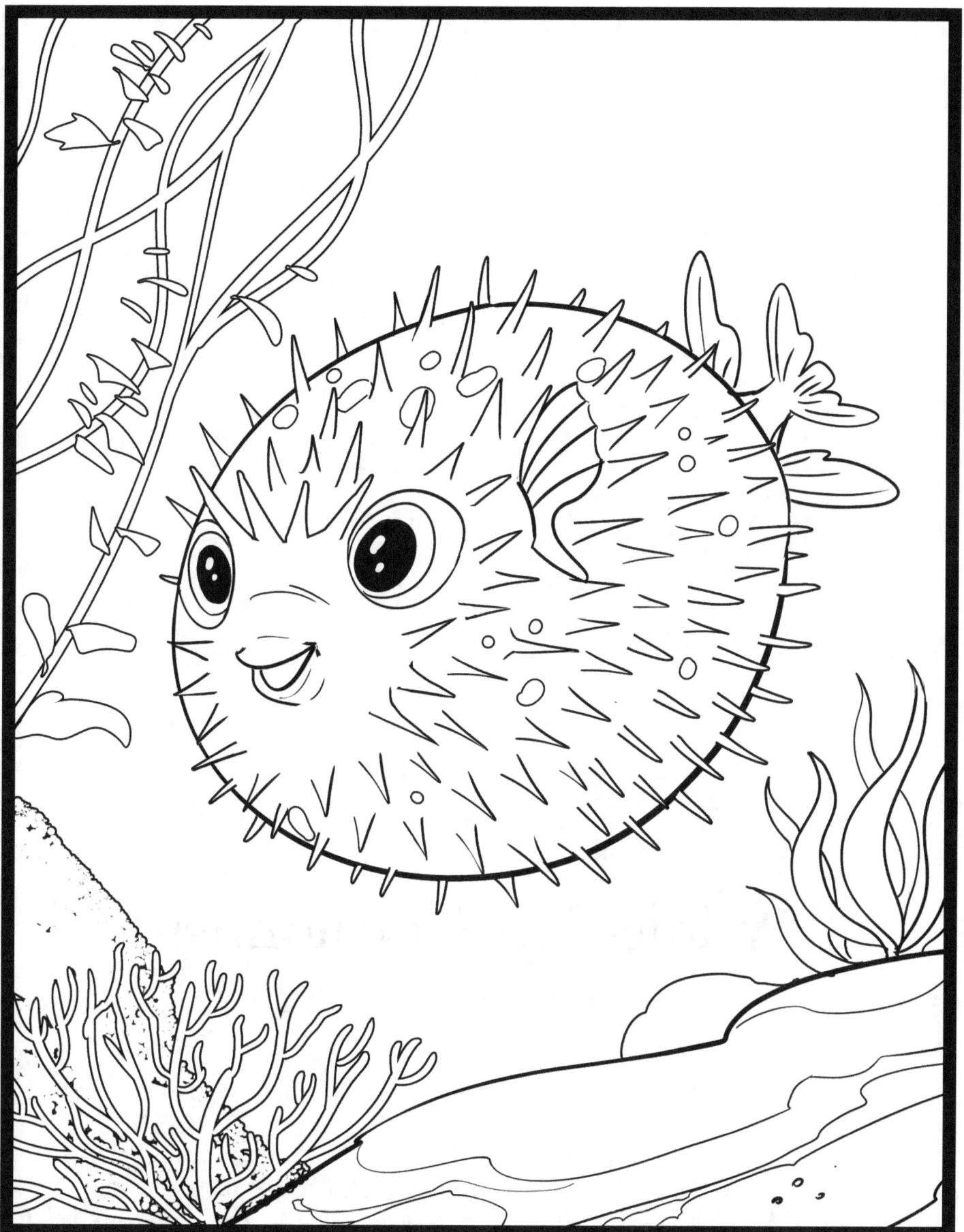

Paddle-flap Scorpionfish
Master of the camouflage.

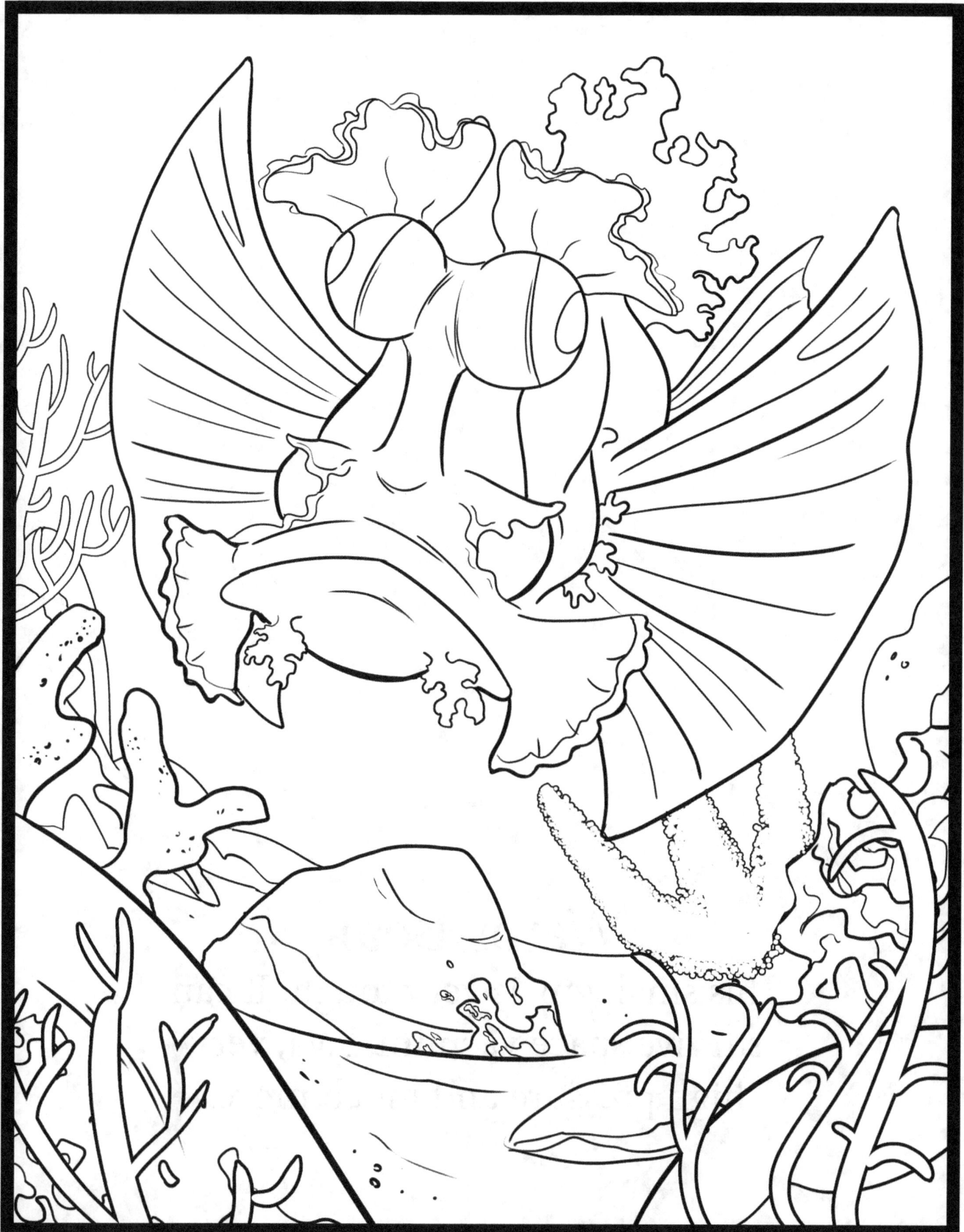

Water Bear

This small guy is very tough. It can survive space vacuum, lava, very high pressure and much more.

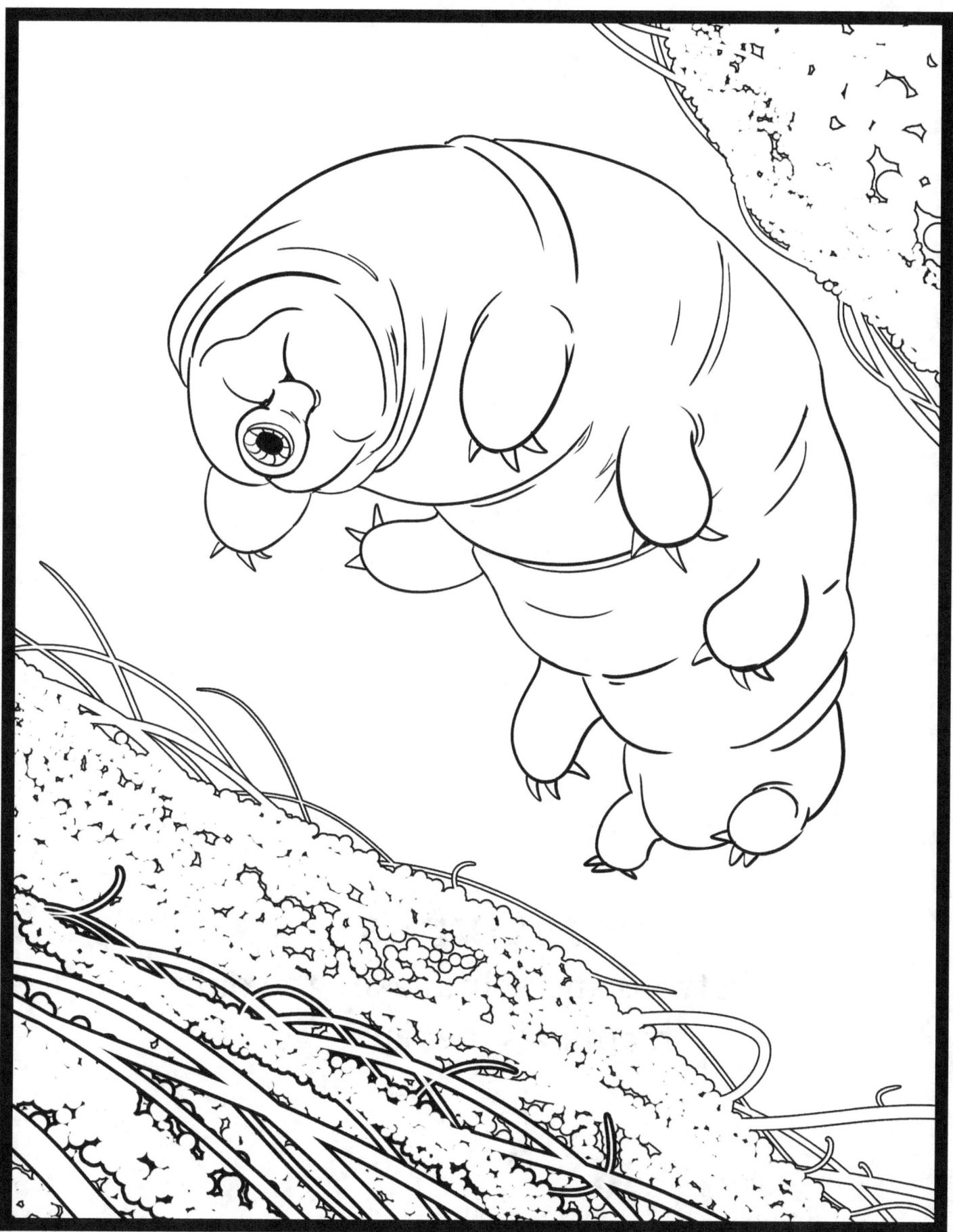

Platypus

Platypus and echidna are the only mammals that lay eggs.

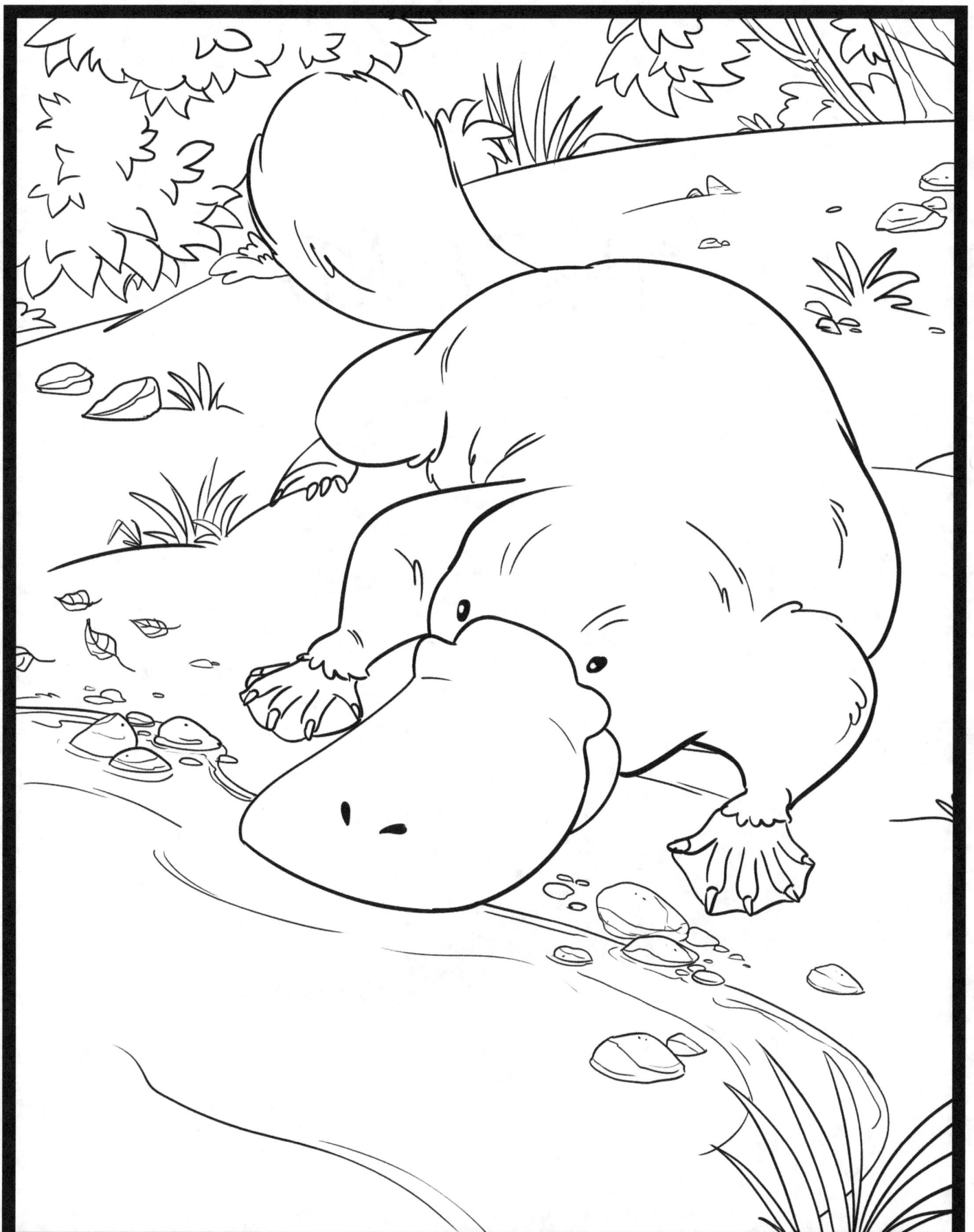

THE END

©2020 Dariusz Radecki
All Rights Reserved